FILL IN THE BLANK FOR KIDS WORKBOOK

Grade 1 - 3 Edition

BABY PROFESSOR

EDUCATION KIDS

Speedy Publishing LLC

40 E. Main St. #1156

Newark, DE 19711

www.speedypublishing.com

Copyright 2016

Vocabulary Exercises

Cut and Paste

Name: _____ Score: _____

Fill in the blanks with the correct letter. Cut and paste the images beside the words.

1. Z_br_

2. J_m

3. C_ndl_

4. Y_rn

For Cutting Purposes Only

Name: _____ Score: _____

Fill in the blanks with the correct letter. Cut and paste the images beside the words.

1. __nt

2. __llig__tor

3. v__n

4. __gg

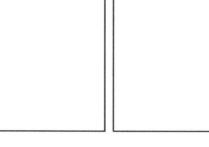

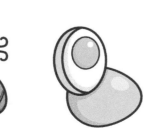

For Cutting Purposes Only

Name: _____ Score: _____

Fill in the blanks with the correct letter. Cut and paste the images beside the words.

1. P_ncil

2. Rock_t

3. Not_

4. Or_ng_

For Cutting Purposes Only

Name: _____ Score: _____

Fill in the blanks with the correct letter. Cut and paste the images beside the words.

1. Y_cht

2. L_mp

3. Xylophon_

4. Wh_l_

For Cutting Purposes Only

Name: _____   Score: _____

Fill in the blanks with the correct letter. Cut and paste the images beside the words.

1. fi_h

2. ba_

3. vas_

4. g_ft

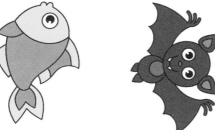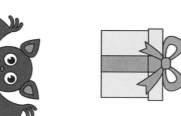

For Cutting Purposes Only

Name: _____   Score: _____

Fill in the blanks with the correct letter. Cut and paste the images beside the words.

1. dr _ m

2. r _ bo _

3. que _ _

4. _ oc _ s

For Cutting Purposes Only

Name: _____ Score: _____

Fill in the blanks with the correct letter. Cut and paste the images beside the words.

1. lad _ b _ g

2. _ ird

3. pe _ ut

4. ro _ k _ t

For Cutting Purposes Only

Name: _____ Score: _____

Fill in the blanks with the correct letter. Cut and paste the images beside the words.

1. hou_e

2. ju_c_

3. i_lo_

4. i_e cre_

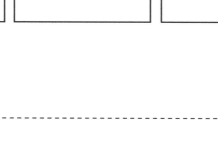

Name: _____   Score: _____

Fill in the blanks with the correct letter. Cut and paste the images beside the words.

1. mou_e

2. isla_d

3. s_u_sh

4.to__to

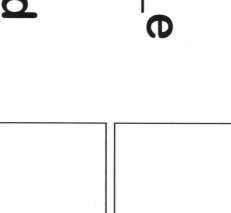
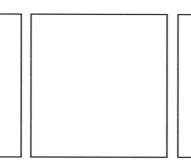

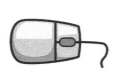

For Cutting Purposes Only

Fill in the blanks

Exercise No. 1

Name: _____   Score: _____

Fill in the blanks with the correct letter.

1. bro ___

2. blo ___

3. cr ___

4. dr ___

5. tr ___

6.  fr ___

Name: _____   Score: _____

Fill in the blanks with the correct letter.

1.  ch __ se

2.  cl __ n

3.  sc __ ol

4.   b __ t

5.  back __ e

6.   br __ in

Name: _____   Score: _____

Fill in the blanks with the correct letter.

1.  gra___

2.  glo___

3.  pret___l

4.  sca___

5.  ska___

6.  slipp___

Name: _____ Score: _____

Fill in the blanks with the correct letter.

1. pho___

2. kni___

3. que___

4. w___ch

5. ri___

6. ___ll

Name: _____   Score: _____

Fill in the blanks with the correct letter.

1. ____ug

4. ____ock

2. ____ench

5. ____ugh

3. ____ck

6. ____uirrel

Name: _____ Score: _____

Fill in the blanks with the correct letter.

1.  _____ etzel

2. _____ ug

3. _____ ess

4. _____ irt

5. _____ hool

6. _____ arf

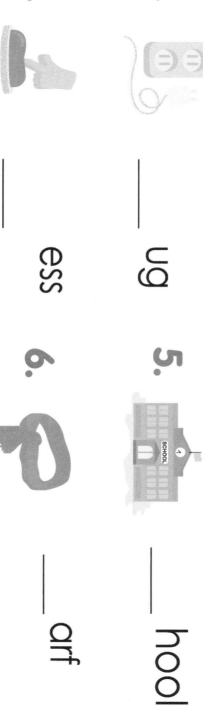

Name: _____ Score: _____

Fill in the blanks with the correct letter.

1.  ____ane

2. ____ume

3.  ____incess

4. 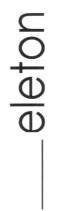 ____eleton

5.  ____an

6.  ____ig

Name: _____   Score: _____

Fill in the blanks with the correct letter.

1.  ____ ock

4. ____ ayon

2.  ____ ain

5.  ____ ock

3.  ____ own

6. ____ oud

Name: _____ Score: _____

Fill in the blanks with the correct letter.

1.  _____ anket

2.  _____ ue

3.  _____ ush

4. _____ ab

5.  _____ own

6. _____ ean

Name: _____   Score: _____

Fill in the blanks with the correct letter.

1.  _____ ozen

2.  _____ ag

3.  _____ uit

4.  _____ obe

5.  _____ ove

6. _____ ape

Name: _____ Score: _____

Fill in the blanks with the correct letter.

1.  ____ og

2.  ____ ower

3. ____ y

4.  ____ ocery

5. ____ ass

6. ____ ass

Fill in the blanks

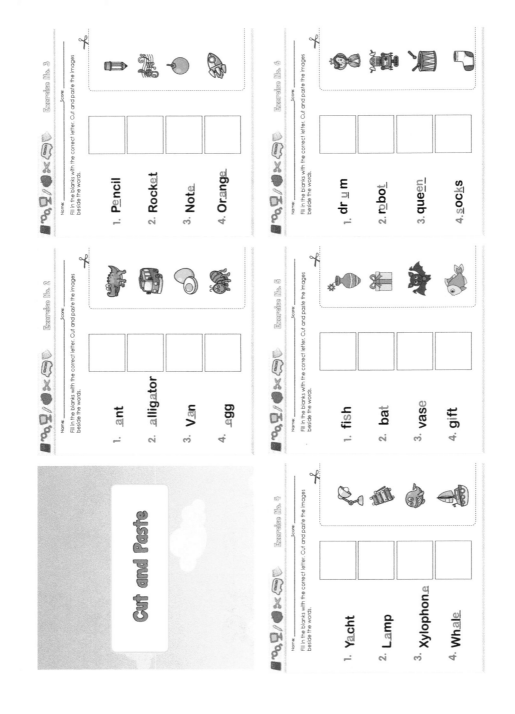

Cut and Paste

Exercise No. 3

Name: _____ Score: _____

Fill in the blanks with the correct letter. Cut and paste the images beside the words.

1. P_e ncil
2. Rocket
3. Note_
4. Orange_

Exercise No. 6

Name: _____ Score: _____

Fill in the blanks with the correct letter. Cut and paste the images beside the words.

1. dr_u m
2. r_o bot_
3. quee_n_
4. _socks

Exercise No. 2

Name: _____ Score: _____

Fill in the blanks with the correct letter. Cut and paste the images beside the words.

1. _ant
2. alligator
3. V_an
4. _egg

Exercise No. 5

Name: _____ Score: _____

Fill in the blanks with the correct letter. Cut and paste the images beside the words.

1. fish
2. bat
3. vase
4. gift

Exercise No. 4

Name: _____ Score: _____

Fill in the blanks with the correct letter. Cut and paste the images beside the words.

1. Y_acht
2. Lamp
3. Xylophon_e
4. Wh_ale

Name: _____ Score: _____

Fill in the blanks with the correct letter. Cut and paste the images beside the words.

1. lad_y_b_u_g

2. b_ird

3. pe_an_ut

4. ro_ck_et

✂

Name: _____ Score: _____

Fill in the blanks with the correct letter. Cut and paste the images beside the words.

1. hou_s_e

2. ju_i_c_e

3. i_glo_o

4. i_c_e cream

✂

Name: _____ Score: _____

Fill in the blanks with the correct letter. Cut and paste the images beside the words.

1. mou_s_e

2. isla_n_d

3. s_qu_a_sh

4. to_m_ato

✂

Fill in the blanks

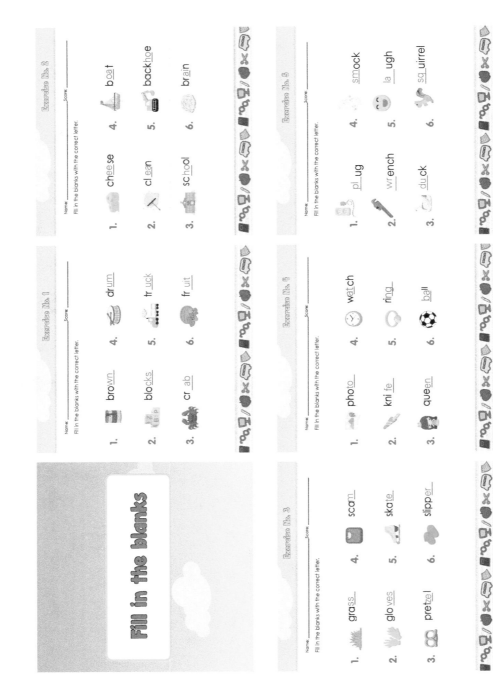

Name: _____ Score: _____

Fill in the blanks with the correct letter.

1. brown
2. blocks
3. cr_ab
4. dr_um
5. tr_uck
6. fr_uit

Name: _____ Score: _____

Fill in the blanks with the correct letter.

1. chee_se
2. cl_ean
3. sc_hool
4. b_oat
5. back_hoe
6. br_ain

Name: _____ Score: _____

Fill in the blanks with the correct letter.

1. gra_ss
2. glo_ves
3. pret_zel
4. sca_n
5. ska_te
6. slipper_

Name: _____ Score: _____

Fill in the blanks with the correct letter.

1. photo_
2. kni_fe
3. que_en
4. wa_tch
5. ring_
6. ball_

Name: _____ Score: _____

Fill in the blanks with the correct letter.

1. pl_ug
2. wr_ench
3. du_ck
4. smock
5. la_ugh
6. sq_uirrel

Name: _____ Score: _____

Fill in the blanks with the correct letter.

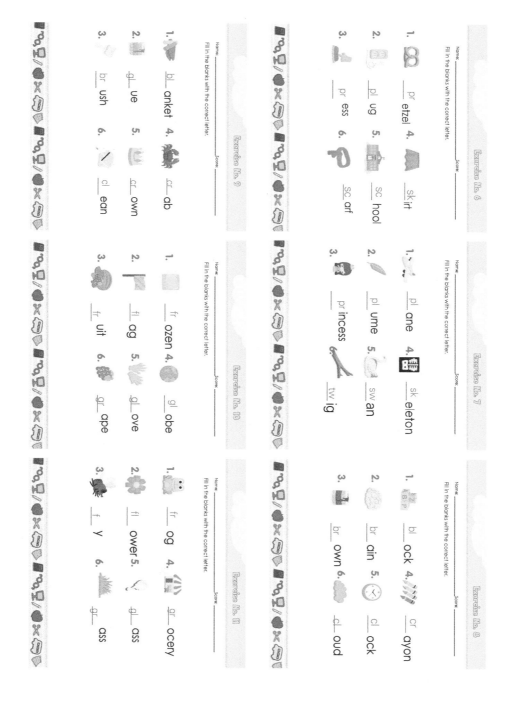

1. _pr_ etzel
2. _pl_ ug
3. _pr_ ess
4. _sk_ irt
5. _sc_ hool
6. _sc_ arf

Name: _____ Score: _____

Fill in the blanks with the correct letter.

1. _bl_ anket
2. _gl_ ue
3. _br_ ush
4. _cr_ ab
5. _gr_ own
6. _cl_ ean

Name: _____ Score: _____

Fill in the blanks with the correct letter.

1. _pl_ ane
2. _pl_ ume
3. _pr_ incess
4. _sk_ eleton
5. _sw_ an
6. _tw_ ig

Name: _____ Score: _____

Fill in the blanks with the correct letter.

1. _bl_ ock
2. _br_ ain
3. _br_ own
4. _cr_ ayon
5. _cl_ ock
6. _cl_ oud

Name: _____ Score: _____

Fill in the blanks with the correct letter.

1. _fr_ ozen
2. _fl_ ag
3. _fr_ uit
4. _gl_ obe
5. _gl_ ove
6. _gr_ ape

Name: _____ Score: _____

Fill in the blanks with the correct letter.

1. _fr_ og
2. _fl_ ower
3. _f_ y
4. _gr_ ocery
5. _gl_ ass
6. _gr_ ass

CPSIA information can be obtained
at www.ICGtesting.com
Printed in the USA
BVHW06083529072 2
643138BV00005B/447